PRESIDENT

by Jacqueline Laks Gorman

Reading consultant: Susan Nations, M.Ed., author/literacy coach/consultant

Please visit our web site at: www.earlyliteracy.cc
For a free color catalog describing Weekly Reader® Early Learning Library's list of high-quality books, call 1-877-445-5824 (USA) or 1-800-387-3178 (Canada). Weekly Reader® Early Learning Library's fax: (414) 336-0164.

Library of Congress Cataloging-in-Publication Data

Gorman, Jacqueline Laks, 1955-
President / by Jacqueline Laks Gorman.
p. cm. – (Our government leaders)
Includes bibliographical references and index.
ISBN 0-8368-4571-4 (lib. bdg.)
ISBN 0-8368-4578-1 (softcover)
1. Presidents–United States–Juvenile literature. I. Title. II. Series.
JK517.G67 2005
352.23'0973–dc22 2004043138

This edition first published in 2005 by
Weekly Reader® Early Learning Library
330 West Olive Street, Suite 100
Milwaukee, WI 53212 USA

Editor: Barbara Kiely Miller
Cover and layout design: Melissa Valuch
Photo research: Diane Laska-Swanke

Photo credits: Cover, title, © Alex Wong/Getty Images; p. 5 © Tim Sloan/AFP/Getty Images; p. 6 © EyeWire; p. 7 © Walter Bennett/Time & Life Pictures/Getty Images; pp. 9, 16 Courtesy Ronald Reagan Library; p. 10 George Bush Presidential Library; p. 11 Cecil Stoughton/Lyndon Baines Johnson Library and Museum; p. 12 © Mark Wilson/Getty Images; p. 13 © Tel Or Beni/GPO/Getty Images; p. 15 © Don Heiny/Weekly Reader; p. 17 © Joe Raedle/Getty Images; p. 19 © Stock Montage, Inc.; p. 20 © North Wind Picture Archives; p. 21 © Marie Hansen/Time & Life Pictures/Getty Images

Printed in the United States of America

1 2 3 4 5 6 7 8 9 09 08 07 06 05

Cover Photo: George W. Bush was elected the forty-third president of the United States in 2000. Before becoming president, he was governor of Texas.

TABLE OF CONTENTS

Who Is the President?

The president is the leader of the United States. He is a leader in the world, too. The president is very powerful. People remember what presidents do for many years.

Adult Americans vote for the president. The president works for all of us. He makes sure that people keep the laws. He also leads the military. People in the military protect the country.

In 2004, President George W. Bush was elected for the second time. He gave a victory speech after he won.

The president lives in the White House. The White House is at 1600 Pennsylvania Avenue in Washington, D.C.

Washington, D.C., is the capital of the United States. The capital is the center of government. The president and his family live there. They live in the White House. The president works there, too. He works in a room called the **Oval Office**.

Trained people protect the president and his family. These guards are called the **Secret Service**.

The president is paid well to do his job. The president travels on a special plane called *Air Force One*. He also has a helicopter.

Presidents often travel on a helicopter called *Marine One*. Jimmy Carter and his wife used it to take a trip together.

What Does the President Do?

The president is the head of the strongest country in the world. His job is one of the biggest and hardest in the world. The president picks many men and women to help him do his job.

The president's top helpers are called his **cabinet**. Members of the cabinet run fifteen government departments. Some departments work with education, health, and farming. The president meets with the people in the cabinet often. They talk about how to fix problems.

When he was president, Ronald Reagan met with his cabinet members to talk about the country's problems.

President George H. W. Bush signed a law in 1990 to help people with disabilities.

Congress is the group of people who make the laws. They represent the people of the fifty states. Sometimes the president wants a new law. He asks Congress to pass the law. He signs the laws. The president may not like a law that Congress has passed. Then he can stop it, or veto it.

The government spends a lot of money every year. Together, the president and Congress decide how to spend the money. Every year, the president gives an oral report, or **address**, to Congress and the people. His report tells everyone how the country is doing.

As president, Lyndon Johnson gave yearly reports to Congress. He told how the country was doing.

At press conferences, presidents talk to reporters. President Bill Clinton enjoyed telling reporters about his ideas.

The president chooses judges to help keep the laws in our country. He chooses **ambassadors** to represent the country in other places. The Senate, which is part of Congress, votes on the people the president picks. The Senate may not agree with the president. Then he must pick someone else.

How should the United States work with other countries? The president decides. He can make agreements with them. This kind of agreement is called a **treaty**. The Senate votes on each treaty.

President Jimmy Carter (*center*) met with the leaders of Egypt and Israel in 1978. He helped them make peace between their countries.

How Does a Person Get to Be President?

The law says that the president must be at least thirty-five years old. He or she must have been born in the United States. He or she must be a citizen. We vote for the president every four years. A person can be president only two times.

Many people want to be president. They talk to citizens, or **campaign**, for months. They have different ideas. People with the same ideas belong to groups called **political parties**. The two main parties hold big meetings, or **conventions**. At the conventions, parties pick their candidates.

At the 2004 Democratic convention, the people cheered for their candidate, John Kerry, and his wife Teresa.

While running for president in 1984, Ronald Reagan (*left*) and Walter Mondale (*right*) had a debate about their ideas.

The candidates travel across the country. They talk to voters. They give speeches. They have debates. Each candidate shares how he or she feels about important issues. Finally, November comes. Election Day is in November.

People all over the country vote. One candidate gets the most votes. He or she is elected president. In January, the new president takes over. The new president moves into the White House with his or her family.

People all over the country vote for the president on Election Day.

Famous Presidents

Many presidents were great men. They led the nation through hard times. They became part of history. A woman has not become president yet.

George Washington became the first president in 1789 when the United States was a new country. Later presidents followed many of the things he did.

Thomas Jefferson was the third president. He had great ideas. He helped shape the country.

Andrew Jackson was the seventh president. He came from a poor family. The people thought he was just like them.

George Washington was a hero of the Revolutionary War. He became the first president of the United States.

© North Wind Picture Archives

President Abraham Lincoln made many speeches that helped the people stay strong during the Civil War.

Abraham Lincoln led the nation during the Civil War. He ended slavery. He was a brave leader when the nation needed him.

A man killed Lincoln in 1865. Three other presidents have been killed, too.

Franklin Roosevelt became president in 1933. Many people were poor and had no jobs. He helped them and gave the country hope.

John Kennedy became president in 1961. People were sad when he was killed in 1963.

President Franklin Roosevelt often talked to the people on the radio. He led the country through World War II.

Glossary

ambassadors – people who are sent to other countries to represent the U.S. government

campaign – to take part in organized activities in order to get elected

candidates – people who seek or are selected by others for an office or honor

citizen – an official member of a country who is given certain rights, such as voting and freedom of speech. A citizen also has duties, such as paying taxes.

debates – discussions of people's different ideas and why they are for or against something

judges – people who listen to and make decisions about cases in a court of law

Senate – one of the two parts of Congress

For More Information

Books

Don't Know Much About the Presidents. Kenneth C. Davis (HarperCollins)

If I Were President. Catherine Stier (Albert Whitman & Company)

The U.S. Presidency. First Facts: Our Government (series). Muriel L. Dubois (Capstone Press)

Web Sites

Ben's Guide to U.S. Government for Kids

bensguide.gpo.gov

A guide to the national government, including the presidency and the rest of the executive branch

The White House for Kids

www.whitehouse.gov/kids

Biographies of the president and first lady, a tour of the White House, and more

INDEX

ABOUT THE AUTHOR

Jacqueline Laks Gorman is a writer and editor. She grew up in New York City. She has worked on many kinds of books and has written several children's series. She lives with her husband, David, and children, Colin and Caitlin, in DeKalb, Illinois. She always votes in every election.